The Middle Ages 1066–1500

John D Clare

Contents

D0488342

Nelson

1066

The Last Viking Invasion

In January 1066 Edward the Confessor, King of England, died. He did not have a son to be king after him. In those days, this meant
5 that there would be a war to see who would be the next king.

Three men claimed the crown:
• Harold Godwinson, the popular Saxon Earl of Wessex;
10 • King Harald Hardrada of Norway, a Viking and the best warrior of the age;
• William, Duke of Normandy.

The Struggle for the Throne

The day after Edward died, Harold
15 Godwinson quickly crowned himself king. But he knew that he would have to fight for his crown. He had a bodyguard of good fighters (called the 'housecarls'). He also called up
20 a large army of ordinary men (this army was called the 'fyrd'). His warships waited in the English Channel.

He waited all summer. Then, on 8 September, his money ran out. 25 He had to send the fyrd home, and call back the fleet to London. On the way back, his ships were destroyed in a storm.

Then worse news reached Harold 30 Godwinson. Harald Hardrada had invaded Yorkshire. Also, one of Godwinson's brothers, Tostig, was helping the Vikings! Godwinson was not worried. When he was told that 35 Hardrada had come to conquer England, he said: 'I will give him just two metres of English soil; enough for his grave.'

Godwinson gathered an army 40 and marched north. He travelled the 200 miles from London to York in only five days. Hearing that Hardrada was only two hours' march away, he gave his men only 45 one hour's rest, and set off to take the Vikings by surprise.

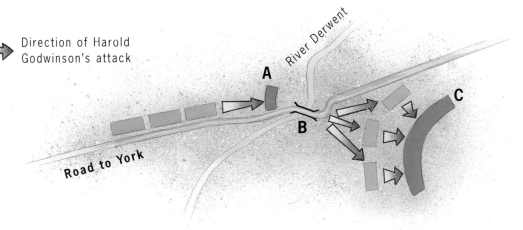

A Harald Hardrada's delaying force
B Bridge
C Harald Hardrada's battle position

→ Direction of Harold Godwinson's attack

A map of the battle of Stamford Bridge, 25 September 1066.

Hardrada's army was about ten miles from York, beside the River Derwent, at a place called Stamford Bridge. Suddenly, Hardrada noticed a cloud of dust – Godwinson's army. He did not have time to draw up his soldiers in proper battle order. What could he do?

Hardrada made a plan. Half of his men would stay on the west bank of the river, to hold up Godwinson and give the rest of his army time to line up properly on the other side of the river.

The Battle

Godwinson attacked. Hardrada's men were driven into the river, and drowned as they tried to swim across it. Hardrada's plan had failed. All Godwinson had to do was to cross the bridge and the battle was won.

But it was not so easy. One brave Viking stood alone on the bridge. He killed every Saxon who tried to go across it. A Saxon soldier found an old wash-tub, and used it to paddle across the river and get behind the brave warrior. The hero was killed, and Godwinson crossed the river.

But by now the Vikings were ready. They had made a strong line called a shield wall.

The Saxons charged. The air was filled with the clash of swords and the cries of the dying. But the Saxons could not break the Vikings' shield wall, and they fell back to take a rest.

After a little while, Godwinson charged again. But this time, his housecarls did not charge. Only the fyrd ran forward and – after a short battle – they turned and ran away.

The Vikings thought they had won. They broke their line, and chased after the Saxon soldiers.

Suddenly, they found themselves in a trap. The fyrd had turned and were fighting back. And Godwinson's housecarls had moved round and were attacking them from behind. There was a great battle, but the Vikings were defeated. Hardrada was killed by an arrow that hit him in the throat, and Tostig was also killed.

A modern photograph of actors showing what a battle between Saxons and Vikings was like.

Harald Hardrada

Harald Hardrada was a legend even in his own lifetime. These stories were told about him:

1 Harald Hardrada as a child

Three brothers – Guttorm, Halfdan and Harald – were playing in a puddle with model boats. King Olaf and the boys' mother sat watching.

King Olaf called Guttorm and Halfdan to him, and he asked Guttorm:
5 'What do you want most?' Guttorm said: 'A cornfield! The whole field over there, jutting out into the lake.'
   'There would be a lot of corn there!' said the king.

Then the king asked Halfdan: 'And what would you most like to have?'
   He said: 'Cows! So many, that when they go down to drink, they'll stand
10 all round the lake, side by side.'
   'That would be a very big farm,' said the king.

Then the king said to Harald: 'And what do you want most of all?'
   'Soldiers!' said Harald. 'So many that they will eat all Halfdan's cows at one meal!'
15   The king laughed and said: 'You are bringing up a king here, mother!'

Snorri Sturluson, *Harald Hardrada's Saga (written in about 1220)*

2 Harald Hardrada dies at Stamford Bridge, 1066

As the battle began, King Harald made up a poem:
      'In battle we should never
      hide behind a shield . . . .
      My armour tells me: "Hold your head up,
5   *where sword meets skull."'*
He got very angry and ran in front of his men.
The Saxons ran away from him.
An arrow hit him in the chin, but he pulled it out.
Another arrow hit him in the throat.
10 Then he sat down.
A friend asked him if he was hurt.
Harald said: 'It's just a small arrow, but it is doing its job.'
And then he died.

Snorri Sturluson, *Harald Hardrada's Saga (written in about 1220)*

Harold Godwinson

It is difficult to know what Harold was really like, because the people who wrote about him were 'biased' (those who were on his side wrote nice things about him, and those who were against him wrote bad things about him).

1 One opinion of Harold Godwinson

Harold began to get rid of bad laws.
He made new good laws.
He helped the Church, and he was kind to bishops and monks.
He loved God. He was not proud.
He was the friend of all good men,
but he was the enemy of all bad men.

Florence of Worcester (died 1118)

2 Another opinion of Harold Godwinson

Harold was a proud, cruel bully – a hateful, bad ruler
who ruined you and made you slaves!

William of Poitiers (c. 1071)

3 Harold Godwinson the lifesaver

A scene from the Bayeux tapestry (c. 1067–70). The tapestry tells the story of how Harold helped William of Normandy during a battle, and did the brave deed shown in the picture below.
  The Latin words mean: 'Here they are crossing the River Cosnon. Here Earl Harold pulls the men from the quicksand.'

Holy Bones

Most of the writers of the time tell the strange story of Harold and the holy bones.

The Bayeux tapestry tells it in picture form.

According to the tapestry, King Edward sent Harold Godwinson on a mission to Normandy in 1064. Harold set sail, but was shipwrecked in a storm. He was captured and imprisoned by a local nobleman.

William, the Duke of Normandy, rescued Harold. Harold stayed with William. He saved Norman soldiers from the quicksand (see page 5). He fell in love with William's daughter.

Then the tapestry shows this picture:

1 Harold's promise
A scene from the Bayeux tapestry (c. 1067–70). The Latin words at the top mean: 'Where Harold makes an oath to Duke William.' An oath is a solemn promise. Harold is touching boxes in which were kept the holy bones of Christian saints.

Did Harold make a promise to Duke William, and if so, what promise did he make? Norman writers were certain they knew what Harold had promised:

2 The Deeds of William of Normandy

Harold was taken to the town of Rouen, in France. Everybody was very happy . . . .

There, Harold promised to be loyal to Duke William. He promised to do everything he could to help the Duke become king of England.

Harold swore on the holy bones in a proper church service. The most truthful men were there, and they say that he made the promise of his own free will.

Written by **William of Poitiers**, *a Norman.*

Saxon writers looked at things differently:

3 The New History of England

William kept Harold with him in France for many days.

During that time he told him what he wanted.

He said: 'If you promise to help me become king . . . you can marry my daughter . . . and I will give you everything you ask for.'

Harold saw that he was in danger. He could not see any way of escape unless he agreed to everything William wanted. So he agreed.

To make sure of the promise, William had bones of the saints brought and he made Harold swear his oath on them.

Written by **Eadmer**, *a Saxon.*

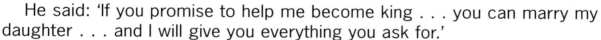

?????? QUESTIONS ???????

The Anglo-Saxon Chronicle was a record of all the events of the time, written down as they happened. It was written by Saxon monks for the kings of England.

The Anglo-Saxon Chronicle does not mention the year 1064 at all. It is the only year not recorded between 1027 and 1132.

1 Can you suggest reasons why *The Anglo-Saxon Chronicle* does not mention the events of 1064?

2 Does this affect your opinion of what happened in Normandy in 1064?

A Bitter Death

King Edward would have preferred to be a monk rather than a king. He was not a great warrior. He could not control his nobles. After 1052, he let Harold Godwinson fight his wars for him. Earl Harold became very important – the 'under-king' of England.

On 28 December 1065, Edward opened a new church which he had built. Eight days later, on 5 January 1066, he suddenly died.

1 King Edward

Now did Edward, Lord of the English,
Send his godly soul to Christ.
Here in the world he lived for a time
In royal majesty, wise in his thinking,
5 A gentle ruler for 24 years, ruler of warriors . . . .
Ever cheerful was the blameless king,
A king of great goodness, pure and kind,
Until suddenly came that bitter death.

Yet did the wise king give his kingdom
10 To a man of high rank, to Harold Godwinson himself,
The noble earl who always obeyed his lord.

The Anglo-Saxon Chronicle for the year 1066

2 King Edward is buried

A scene from the Bayeux tapestry (c. 1067–70). The Latin words mean: 'Here is carried the body of King Edward.' The scene shows the church Edward built. Today it is called Westminster Abbey.

King Harold Godwinson

When Edward died, Harold immediately seized the throne. The picture below shows King Harold with the Saxon noblemen, and Archbishop Stigand, who crowned Harold king.

A scene from the Bayeux tapestry. The Latin words mean: 'Here sits Harold, king of the English.'

Duke William Invades

William of Normandy was very angry when he heard that Harold Godwinson had seized the throne. He began to gather an army to invade England.

1 William's men cutting trees.

2 Using the wood to build boats.

3 The Latin words mean: 'Here they drag the ships to the sea.'

4 'These men carry arms to the ships: and here they drag a wagon with wine and with weapons.'

5 Duke William crosses the sea, and comes to Pevensey [on the south coast of England].

6 'Here the war-horses leave the ships.'

7 'Here the soldiers go to Hastings to steal food.'

8 'William orders that a castle be built at Hastings.'

9 'Here a house is burned.'

The Battle of Hastings, 1066

1 Norman messengers.

William's army was ready to sail on 12 August 1066, but a strong wind kept him in port for six weeks. William did not land in England
5 until 28 September, a few days after Godwinson had defeated Hardrada at Stamford Bridge. The Normans stole food, burned houses and killed English people.

10 Harold was so angry when he heard what William was doing that he ignored advice to let his men rest. He marched south in only seven days. He tired out his army.

15 Near Hastings, Harold stopped to let his men sleep. William left Hastings, and took Harold by surprise.

Harold took up a position near an old apple tree on top of a grassy ridge
20 called Senlac Hill, near Hastings. He put his men into a shield wall, and flew his two flags – the Dragon of Wessex and the Fighting Man of the family Godwin. His orders were
25 simple: 'HOLD FAST THE LINE.'

2 Some of the knights who formed William's cavalry (soldiers on horseback).

3 Norman archers.

The Battle of Hastings

On the morning of 14 October 1066, William ordered his infantry (foot-soldiers) to attack. But their arrows bounced harmlessly off the English
30 shields, and the Norman soldiers turned and ran. A rumour went round that William was dead. The Duke had to take off his helmet and ride amongst his men to stop them running
35 away. Both sides rested and ate.

4 'Here is Duke William.'

In the afternoon, William sent in his cavalry. Ivo Taillefer, a brave knight, galloped out in front, juggling his sword and lance in the air. The
40 knights rode up the hill and crashed onto the English shield wall.

But the great war-horses could not gather enough speed up the hill. Ivo Taillefer was hacked to pieces. Many
45 soldiers on both sides were killed, including Harold's two brothers, Gurth and Leofwine. The Normans could not break the English line, however.

50 Yet just as it seemed that Harold was going to win, disaster struck. The Normans turned and pretended to run away. The English fyrd broke the line and chased after them. William's
55 cavalry turned and cut them to pieces. The rest of the fyrd ran away.

The Death of Harold Godwinson

The housecarls refused to run away, however. They formed a ring round their king. William ordered his
60 archers to shoot high. Harold was killed. Time after time the Norman cavalry thundered down upon their shield wall. After each attack the ring was smaller, but the housecarls did
65 not surrender.

The Normans killed them all. Then they chased and butchered the fleeing fyrd-men until midnight.

The kingdom belonged to William.

5 Norman cavalry attack the English shield wall.

6 Norman knights charging up a hill.

7 Norman knights cut down English soldiers on level ground.

8 'And the English turn and run away.'

How Did Harold Die?

Most people will tell you that Harold Godwinson died because he was hit in the eye by an arrow. They are probably wrong. They believe this because of this picture from the Bayeux tapestry:

1 This detail from the Bayeux tapestry (*c.* 1067–70) is the best-known picture of the death of Harold. The Latin words mean: 'Here King Harold is killed.' This is the picture you will see in most history books.

? ? ? ? ? ? ? ? ? ? QUESTIONS ? ? ? ? ? ? ? ? ? ? ?

1 Look at source 1. Identify the man who seems to be Harold. How, does it appear, did Harold die?

> But did he? Remember how the battle ended (page 13):
> The housecarls refused to run away. They formed a ring round their king . . . .
> the Norman cavalry thundered down upon their shield wall.

2 Look at source 2. Find the attacking Norman cavalry. Find the two sides of the housecarls' ring. Identify Harold, the man in the centre of the ring. Now, how does it seem that Harold died?

Source 1, however, does not show the whole scene from the tapestry.

2 The complete scene in the Bayeux tapestry, showing the death of Harold.

45

William the Conqueror

After the battle of Hastings, William was crowned king in London on Christmas Day, 1066.

The Saxons in the north-east of England did not want William as their king. In 1069, they rebelled against him.

5   King William quickly gathered an army, and hurried to Northumberland in great anger, and did not stop for the whole winter from destroying the country and killing the men . . . .

Because of this, there was so great a famine that men, forced by hunger, ate human flesh, that of horses, dogs and cats, and everything
10   that is horrible. It was horrific to see human corpses decaying in the houses, the streets and the roads, swarming with worms, while they rotted with an abominable stench. For no-one was left to bury them, for everyone had either been killed by the sword, or by the famine, or had left the country because of the famine.

15   Meanwhile, the land was deserted. The villages between Durham and York were empty. They became hiding places for wild animals and robbers.

Simeon of Durham, *A History of the Kings.*
Simeon died in 1129.

20   William took absolute control over England. Almost all the Saxons lost their land. William said that ALL the land in England belonged to him. Important Saxon noblemen were reduced to the level of village officials. Ordinary Saxon freemen lost their freedom. They became unpaid workers for the Normans. They were called villeins.

The Domesday Book
25 In 1086, William made a survey of all the land in England. His surveyors wrote down how much land belonged to each village, who had owned it in the time of King Edward the
30 Confessor and who held it now. They also wrote down how many ploughs and villeins there were in each village.

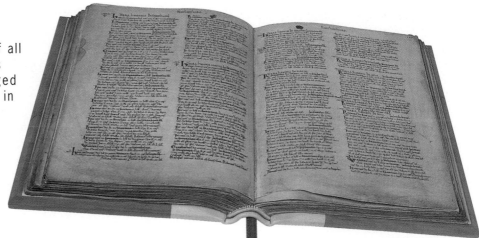

Feudal England

William organised the land in England in a certain way.

William kept one fifth of the land in England for his own royal estates. He gave a quarter of the land to the Church.

The rest of the land he shared out between his Norman followers. There were only about 180 of them.

These Normans were the tenants-in-chief (they were usually barons or bishops).

In return for their land, they took an oath of loyalty to William and promised to provide soldiers or money for William's army.

They kept some land for themselves and split up the rest into manors, which they gave to their followers.

These men were the under-tenants (they were usually knights).

In return for their land, they took an oath of loyalty to the baron and promised to serve as a knight in the army.

They kept some land (called the demesne) for themselves and shared the rest between the Saxon peasants who lived on their manor.

Most Saxons were owned by the lord of the manor; they were villeins.

In return for their land, they had to obey the lord of the manor and give him part of their crops. They also worked without pay on the lord's land.

Villeins were not free men.

This system is known as the Feudal System.

A VILLEIN'S LIFE

What was life like for the villeins who lived in a feudal village? The small village of Middridge in County Durham gives us an idea:

In MIDDRIDGE there are 15 villeins and every one of them holds 30 acres and they give 8 chalders of malt and the same of meal and
5   the same of oats, and 40 chalders of oat-malt and seven and a half cartloads of wood and 30 hens and 1,000 eggs and they pay £2 for their cattle and give 1 milking cow and do duty at the castle, and pay 15 shillings instead of reaping, and 5 shillings instead of waiting at the bishop's table at Christmas, and they work in all ways as the villeins of Heighington.
10   Wekeman holds 60 acres and pays 6 shillings and does 3 boon-works and ploughs 1 day and mows 1 day and carts hay and corn 2 days and supervises the boon-works and goes on the bishop's errands.

Boldon Book (1183), a survey of the lands held by the Bishop of Durham.

chalder: 32 sacks.
15   *malt: barley that has been soaked and roasted, ready to be made into beer.*
meal: grain that has been partly ground, ready to be made into flour.
shilling: 5p – a large amount of money in 1183.
the bishop's table: in Middridge, the Bishop of Durham was the lord of the manor.
as the villeins of Heighington: the villeins of Heighington mowed the meadows, cared for the
20   *orchard, carted corn 'wherever the bishop wanted', gave rope for the bishop's hunt, and worked two days a week on the bishop's land during autumn.*
Wekeman: his name suggests that he was the overseer, who 'woke up' the inhabitants and set them to work. He was a Saxon given extra land so he would help the Normans.
boon-works: extra days of work done for the bishop, whenever he wanted.

25 A village reeve (overseer) supervising workers.

Villeins were completely under the power of the lord of the manor. In return for their land they had to give him part of their crops and work 30 without pay on the lord's land.

A villein also had to pay a *merchet* (so his daughter could marry), and supply free food when the lord's steward arrived to collect the crops. 35 He had to pay the lord of the manor before he could grind corn, brew ale, bake bread, gather wood or sell his animals. He could not fish or hunt except on the Common. 55

A villein owned 'nothing but his own stomach' and was his master's possession. When a villein died, the lord of the manor took a tax called a *heriot* (which included his animals, 60 clothes, pots and possessions) and the Church took a tax called a *mortuary*.

He could not leave the manor without permission. If he did leave, the lord's men hunted him down. 65

The Normans destroyed the Saxon village of Middridge and rebuilt it as two straight rows of 40 huts. In 1183, Middridge was a concentration camp, into which the conquered Saxons had been herded.

The village lands were divided into three huge 'open fields'. Each 45 villein had thirty strips of land scattered around the three fields. One field would grow barley, another would grow oats, and the third was left 50 'fallow' to rest the soil. The following year this was rotated, so that each field was given a rest in turn.

North Field

Barley

MIDDRIDGE

East Field

Oats

South Field

Fallow (uncultivated)

Oxclose
(the meadow)

MIDDRIDGE GRANGE
(the manor house)

The Farming Year

These pictures from *The Luttrell Psalter* (written in about 1340) show work on the estates of Sir Geoffrey Luttrell, an English knight.

A Stacking sheaves of corn.

B Harrowing, to break up the clods of earth and kill the weeds.

C Ploughing with oxen.

20

D Reaping, using a blade called a sickle.

E A harvest cart.

F Villagers had to grind their corn at the lord's mill.

G Sowing the seed.

Pierce the Ploughman

This is a description of a ploughman and his family, written in about 1394. Compare the ploughman in this poem to the one in source C on page 20.

As I went by the way · weeping for sorrow,
I saw a poor man by me · upon the plough hanging.
His coat was of cloth · that rough was called,
His hood was full of holes · and his hair stuck out,
5 With his worn shoes · patched again and again;
His toes hung out · as he trod the earth,
His socks overhung his shoes · on every side,
All beslobbered in mud · as he followed the plough;
Two mittens as mean · made all of patches;
10 The fingers were frayed · and full of mud hung.
This worker wallowed in the mud · almost to the ankle,
Four oxen before him · so weak had become;
You could count every rib · so wretched they were.

His wife walked with him · with a long goad,
15 In a coat cut short · cut full high,
Wrapped in a sacking sheet · to shield her from the weather,
Barefoot on the bare ice · that the blood followed.

And at the land's end lay · a little bowl,
And on it lay a little child · wrapped in rags,
20 And two of two years old · on another side,
And they all sang a song · that was sad to hear;
And they all cried a cry · a note full of care.
And the poor man sighed sore and said · 'children, be still!'
Pierce the Ploughman's Crede (c.1394), an anonymous poem.

25 **mean**: *poorly made.*
goad: *a stick used to hit the oxen.*

? ? ? ? ? ? QUESTIONS ? ? ? ? ? ? ? ?

1 How does the reader know that it was wintertime?
2 List all the words in the poem that suggest the ploughman was poor.

A Villein's Home

Very little work could be done in winter. The picture below shows French peasants at home in February. The painting is one of the pictures in a prayer book which belonged to a French lord, the Duc de Berry. The book is called *Les Très Riches Heures* (1416).

Having Fun

Even in summer, people did not work all the time in the Middle Ages. In fact they had many holy days (holidays) – more than one hundred a year!

This painting shows a peasant wedding feast.

These pictures from *The Luttrell Psalter* show some of the ways in which English villagers enjoyed themselves.

1 Piggyback wrestling.

2 Bear-baiting.

3 A performing monkey.

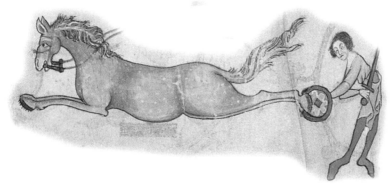

4 Travelling performers.

5 A drinking game.

6 Archery practice – in the fourteenth century people had to practise archery by order of the king.

25

Women in the Middle Ages

Historians disagree about the role of women during the Middle Ages.

Before 1066, women in Saxon England had a great deal of freedom. Some women became very important.

Some historians think that 1066 was a disaster for women – not only villein women, but rich women as well. They think that the Norman Conquest brought a male soldier-class to power, who ignored women and gave them lowly jobs. Other historians say that women were influential and played an important part in society.

The sources on these pages will help *you* to decide what you think.

1 A woman making medicines to heal her husband. How does she know what to do?

2 A lady giving orders to her servants in the kitchen.

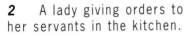

3 A husband beating his wife.

4 A woman and her maid.

5 A wife beating her husband. Many pictures on this theme have survived.

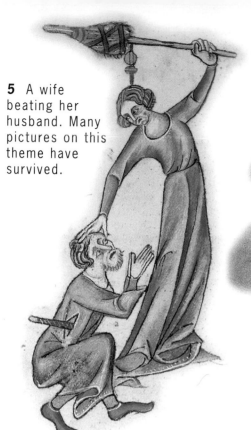

6 A woman spinning.

7 Feeding the hens.

8 A milkmaid.

9 A female blacksmith.

10 Women often had to defend the castle if their husbands were away.

THE CHURCH

In the Middle Ages, people believed that bad people went to hell when they died. This description shows what they thought hell was like:

I saw a great swamp. A black cloud of smoke hung over it and a mass of little worms swarmed all over it. In the swamp were the souls
5   of those who had enjoyed foolish fun when they were alive.

And I saw a great fire, black, red and white, and in it horrible fiery vipers spitting flame; the vipers tortured the souls of those who had been nasty to others.

And I saw a great fire burning in the blackness, and there were dragons in it.
10   Nearby was an icy river. The liars were punished here. To escape the heat, they went into the river. Then, because of the cold, they returned to the fire, and the dragons tormented them.

And I saw the thickest darkness. In it were those people who had not obeyed their bishop. They lay on a fiery pavement and were bitten by sharp-toothed
15   worms.

And I saw high in the air a hail of ice and fire falling . . . and I saw demons with fiery whips beating here and there.

Hildegard of Bingen, *The Book of the Rewards of Life (1171).*
Hildegard of Bingen was an abbess (head of a nunnery).

20   In the Middle Ages people believed that to get to heaven they had to go to church. They believed that only the priest could forgive
25   their sins. This made the Church, and the priest, very important in their lives.

Right: In the Middle Ages, everyone had to give the Church one tenth
30   (a 'tithe') of everything they produced. Here, peasants pay their tithes to the priest. Do you think people enjoyed giving their tithes?

Below: A painting of hell, from the Duc de Berry's *Les Très Riches Heures* (1416). What sort of people went to hell? What happened to them?

What the Church Did

The main job of the Church was to get people to heaven. The priest baptised babies, married young couples, heard confession, gave the
5 last rites to the dying and buried the dead. He gave people the body of Christ (the bread) at the service of the Mass. Women who had given birth were made to attend a service
10 to make them 'clean'.

But the Church did much more than simply hold services. Monasteries and nunneries cared for the old and the sick. They gave alms (money) to
15 poor people, and looked after travellers (often free of charge).

In the Middle Ages, monks were among the few people who could read and write. They were important
20 people. They taught the children of the rich. They copied books and drew up legal documents.

Poor people went to the priest for advice on their personal problems. Abbots and bishops acted as advisers to the king.   35

Few people attacked clerics (churchmen) because they thought God would be angry. As a result, churches and monasteries were safe places. People went there for   40 protection. Criminals could go to a church and claim 'sanctuary' – they could not be arrested. Monasteries and nunneries sometimes acted as banks, and looked after people's   45 money for them.

The Church also helped to entertain people. Church festivals and saints' days were 'holy days', when everybody went to church in the   50 morning – and spent the rest of the day enjoying themselves. Often, the Church held processions, and put on 'miracle plays' which were stories from the Bible acted out in public.   55

Right: A baptism.
25 Many people died young. People believed that it was important to baptise babies
30 quickly, so that they would go to heaven if they died.

A painting of a church service from the Duc de Berry's *Les Très Riches Heures* (1416). It is the Christmas Day Mass. The priest reads the service from a book on the altar. Helping him with the service are two deacons (kneeling beside the altar) and two priests (kneeling behind him). A choir sings, although they have to share the music! Can you see the church organ?

Two rich women follow the service in their own service books. The rest of the people watch from the nave, behind a wooden screen.

Devoted to God

Some men and women decided to devote their whole lives to God. They became monks and nuns. They took vows of poverty (to be poor), obedience (to obey) and chastity (not to marry). There were different kinds of monks and nuns, but most followed the 'threefold rule' and spent their day working, studying and praying.

1 Every morning, the abbot called the monks into the Chapter House and read to them a chapter of the monks' book of rules. Monks who broke the rules were punished.

2 Most monks and nuns went to eight church services every day.

3 The cellarer looked after the monastery bakehouse and the brewhouse. Notice his keys.

4 A monk teaching. Some pupils were novices: children sent to the monastery to become monks. Others were the sons of local lords who wanted them to be able to read and write.

6 Monks at work.

5 The hospitaller gave travellers hospitality in the monastery hospital (guest house). The almoner gave alms to the poor.

7 Monks and nuns ate in the refectory. They often ate in silence while someone read from the Bible. Before each meal, they washed their hands in a room called the lavatorium.

8 Monks and local people who were sick, old or infirm, went to the monastery's infirmary to be looked after.

9 Monks copied books in the cloister.

10 Not all monastery life was dull.

11 Not all monks and nuns were holy. These two have misbehaved and have been put in the stocks.

Thomas à Becket

In the Middle Ages, the Church was very rich and powerful. The Pope – who was head of the Christian Church – claimed that even kings

5 should obey him. The Pope said that if a priest committed a crime, he should be tried in special Church courts, where the punishments were not very strict.

10 But King Henry II of England (1154–89) wanted more control over the Church in England. He wanted priests and monks to be tried by the king's judges.

15 Henry's best friend was a priest called Thomas à Becket. When the Archbishop of Canterbury died in 1162, Henry saw a chance to get more control over the Church. He

20 appointed Thomas as Archbishop of Canterbury.

But when Thomas became 25 Archbishop, he changed. He spent a lot of time praying and reading the Bible. He gave food to the poor and washed their feet. He wore an uncomfortable hair shirt like a monk. 30 When Henry tried to get more control over the Church courts, Becket stopped him.

Eventually, on Christmas Day, 1170, Henry lost his temper. 'Will nobody 35 rid me of this troublesome priest?' he shouted out to no-one in particular.

Thomas à Becket was a proud and boastful man. He had insulted many of Henry's knights. Four of them 40 saw their chance. They went to Canterbury, put on their armour and strode into the Cathedral.

The knights killed Becket (see right). 45

The Pope as ruler of the world. On his right are the abbots, bishops monks, nuns and other clerics (churchmen). On his left are the kings, lords, knights, merchants, peasants and other lay people.

The death of Becket

Full of anger, the knights called out, 'Where is Thomas Becket?' At this, bold and fearless, he answered, 'I am here.' Having said this, he turned to the right, under a pillar, by the altar of the Virgin Mary.

50 Then they laid evil hands on him, dragging him so that they might kill him outside the church. But they could not pull him from the pillar.

Then, seeing that he was about to die, he bowed his head and, joining his hands, he lifted them up and prayed to the Virgin Mary.

He had barely spoken when a wicked knight suddenly leapt on him and wounded him on the head, cutting off the top of his crown; and by the same blow

55 he wounded the arm of him who tells this.

He was given a second blow to the head, but still stood firm. At the third blow he fell to his hands and knees, saying in a low voice, 'For the name of Jesus I am ready to die.'

Then the third knight gave him a terrible wound as he lay there, so that the

60 sword broke against the stone floor and the top of the head was cut right off – so that the blood white with the brain, and the brain red with blood, dyed the floor of the church.

The fourth knight stopped anyone interfering. And a fifth, a cleric who had gone with the knights, put his foot on the neck of the holy priest and, horrible to say,

65 scattered his brains and blood over the floor.

Edward Grim, *writing in about 1176.*
Edward Grim was a monk who wrote his account about six years after Becket's death.
How can we tell that Grim was an eye-witness?

Everybody was angry with Henry.
70 Rumours spread that miracles had happened at Becket's tomb. The Pope made Becket a saint.

In 1174 King Henry walked barefoot through the streets of
75 Canterbury. To show he was sorry about Becket's death, he let the monks whip him. He gave up his attempt to control the Church in England. Becket had won.

80 *Right:* The death of Becket, a painting from about 1300. Compare this painting with Grim's account of Becket's murder.

Pilgrims

In the Middle Ages, priests taught people to believe in purgatory, a place where people's sins were burned out of their souls after they had died. It was said that the fires burning there were as fierce as those in hell.

To please God, and to avoid years of torment in purgatory, people went on a pilgrimage. The most adventurous pilgrims went to Jerusalem, to see the Holy Land where Jesus had lived. Others went to Rome, where the Pope lived (these pilgrims were called 'roamers').

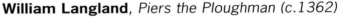

A pilgrim

He carried a staff · with a wide strip of cloth,
Like a bindweed plant · twisted around it.
A bag and a bowl · hung from his belt;
A hundred bottles of holy oil · upon his hat,
And other souvenirs · shells from Spain,
Many a cross on his cloak · and keys from Rome
And a St Veronica handkerchief · so people might know,
And see by these signs · which shrines he had seen.

William Langland, *Piers the Ploughman (c.1362)*

bottles of holy oil: *a sign that he had been to the shrine of Thomas à Becket at Canterbury.*
shells from Spain: *scallop shells from the shrine of St James at Compostela in Spain.*
keys from Rome: *cross-keys were the emblem of St Peter, who was crucified in Rome.*
a St Veronica handkerchief: *the shrine of St Veronica was in Rome. She had lent her veil to Jesus to wipe the sweat from his face before he was crucified.*

1 Two pilgrims. They wear rough clothes and carry staffs. Which shrine have they just visited?

2 Pilgrims being attacked. Ambush and robbery was a common danger on pilgrimage. Pilgrims going to Jerusalem had to travel through Muslim lands. They were often attacked by the Muslims.

3 Many English people went to the shrine of St Thomas at Canterbury in Kent. Pilgrims often travelled in groups, for company and safety.

The Pilgrimage Game

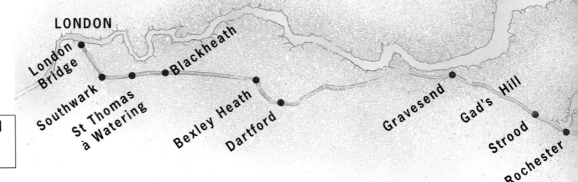

LONDON

London Bridge · Southwark · St Thomas à Watering · Blackheath · Bexley Heath · Dartford · Gravesend · Gad's Hill · Strood · Rochester

1 Start at LONDON

2 LONDON BRIDGE
   a. St Mary's Church
   b. Traitor's Gate
   c Chapel of
      St Thomas

3 SOUTHWARK

4 ST THOMAS À WATERING

5 BLACKHEATH
   a. St Catherine's
      Hermitage
   b. Caesar's Well

6 BEXLEY HEATH

A man on pilgrimage in 1486, walking through woods.

7 End of first day: stop at DARTFORD
   a. The Bull
   b. Spital Street
   c. Holy Trinity
      Church
   d. Trinity Hospital

8 GRAVESEND
   a. Hospital of
      St Thomas
   b. St Mary's Church
   c. Windmill Hill

9 GAD'S HILL
   a. Shrine of
      St Thomas
   b. Danes' Holes
   c. Shrine of
      St Hilderforth

10 STROOD
   a. Pond
   b. Lazar House
   c. St Mary's
      Chapel
   d. Bridge

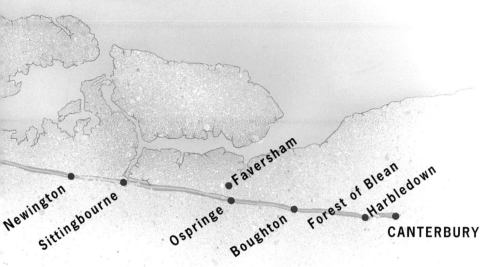

River Thames

Newington
Sittingbourne
Ospringe
Faversham
Boughton
Forest of Blean
Harbledown
CANTERBURY

19 Fifth day: visit CANTERBURY CATHEDRAL
- a. Three statues
- b. Altar
- c. Chapel of Our Lady
- d. Shrine of St Thomas

18 End of fourth day: reach CANTERBURY
- a. The Star
- b. Chapel of St Thomas
- c. St Thomas's Hospital
- d. King's Street
- e. Mercery Lane

17 HARBLEDOWN

16 FOREST OF BLEAN

15 BOUGHTON

A pilgrim sleeping by the roadside.

11 End of second day: stop at ROCHESTER
- a. Shrine of St William
- b. The Cathedral
- c. Crown Inn
- d. St Catherine's Hospital

12 NEWINGTON
- a. Cross
- b. Nunfield Farm
- c. Keycol Hill

13 SITTINGBOURNE
- a. Schamel Hermitage
- b. Chilton Chapel
- c. The Lion Inn

14 End of third day: stop at OSPRINGE
- a. Maison Dieu
- b. Faversham Abbey

The Crusades

Jerusalem was the Holy City of the Christian religion, but it was part of the Turkish empire, and the Turks were Muslims.

5 In 1095, the Pope asked the people of Europe to go on a crusade to conquer the Holy Land for Christianity. Over the next four hundred years, thousands of Christians

10 went to fight the Muslims.

There were many reasons why people went on crusade.

Some were genuinely religious men. The Pope promised all crusaders

15 forgiveness for their sins. This was important for knights who had killed people in battle, and believed that they were going to hell.

Other knights actually went to kill

20 and steal. At home, kings encouraged the most violent nobles to go on crusade, because it got them out of the country!

A drawing of a crusader from the thirteenth century. Some crusaders joined orders of knights such as the Knights of the Hospital of St John, and the Knights Templars. They took vows of poverty and chastity and lived holy lives.

The Hospitallers' order still survives today as the St John's Ambulance Brigade.

To go on a crusade was a great adventure. The Holy Land was full of different sights and unknown goods. Young knights could prove how brave they were. Sometimes the younger son 45 of a great lord – who did not expect to inherit his father's lands – would go on crusade to win land. Villeins joined the crusades, because the Pope promised them freedom if they went 50 to fight.

A map of the crusades.

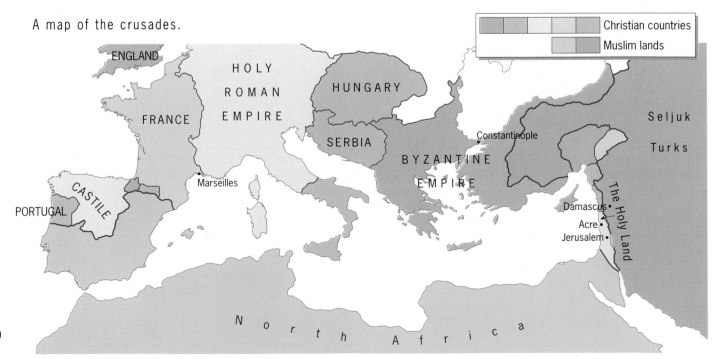

Christian countries
Muslim lands

ENGLAND
HOLY ROMAN EMPIRE
FRANCE
HUNGARY
SERBIA
PORTUGAL
CASTILE
Marseilles
Constantinople
BYZANTINE EMPIRE
Seljuk Turks
Damascus
Acre
Jerusalem
The Holy Land
North Africa

The wars of the crusades were violent and bitter, and both the crusaders and the Muslims were often very cruel. How is this drawing from the fourteenth century different from the drawing of the crusader on page 40?

The Results of the Crusades

In the East, the crusaders discovered all sorts of things they had never seen before, such as lemons, apricots, sugar, silk and cotton. They discovered new spices (used in cooking) and new perfumes. While the crusaders were fighting the Muslims, European merchants were sailing to the Holy Land and trading with the Muslims for these goods!

The crusaders realised that in some ways the Muslims were more civilised than the Europeans. The Muslims knew much more about medicine. They were also better at mathematics: Arabic numbers (1, 2, 3, 4, etc.) were easier to use than Roman numerals (I, II, III, IV, etc.).

The Muslims knew more about geography. In the Holy Land, the crusaders heard about unknown lands in the Far East. In 1275 a European, Marco Polo, visited China. The crusaders realised that the world was a bigger place than they had thought.

The crusades led to improvements in armour and castle design in the West. One Chinese invention that found its way to Europe was gunpowder – a discovery that changed the world.

In 1492, Christopher Columbus (below) tried to find a new way to bring spices from the Far East to western Europe without going through Muslim lands. He used Muslim mathematics to work out the size of the earth, and Muslim geography to find a way to sail west to China. As a result, he discovered America.

1492 is often said to be the date when the Middle Ages came to an end.

THE GOVERNMENT

Henry II and the Law

Before the reign of Henry II (1154–1189), most law cases were decided by the local lord. People who did serious crimes were tried by the king himself. King Henry II changed this. He appointed judges, who went round the country holding courts (called 'assizes'). He also began to rely more on juries, rather than 'trial by ordeal'.

1 *Above:* Before Henry II, people believed in 'trial by ordeal'. Sometimes, a man had to fight the man he accused ('trial by combat'). He won his case only if he won the battle! Sometimes, a man might be told to hold a piece of hot iron. If the burn did not heal quickly, he was found guilty. In 'trial by water', the accused was tied up and thrown into the river. If he floated, he was guilty.

Which was the most unfair method of trial?

2 *Left:* A court in about 1300. Can you find the five judges, the clerks (taking notes), their pens and ink pots, the accused man, the ushers (who kept order – look for their staffs), the other criminals awaiting trial, the lawyers and the jury?

In the Middle Ages, the judge decided whether a person was innocent or guilty. The jury simply acted as witnesses, telling the judges whether they thought the accused was guilty or not. But it was still a fairer system than trial by ordeal.

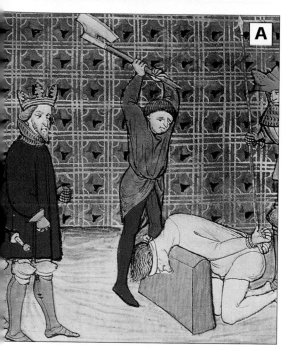

A

Punishments in the Middle Ages were cruel. The pictures A–F show the punishments for fighting, nagging, selling bread that was underweight, trying to kill the king, stealing a cow and rebellion. Can you guess which punishment was given for each crime?

Criminals who escaped became 'outlaws'. England's most famous outlaw is Robin Hood (although most historians doubt whether he ever existed).

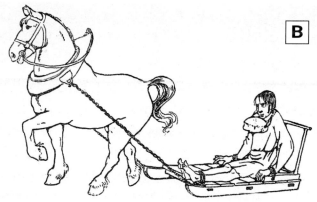

B

C

D

E

F

43

King John

King John (1199–1216) was the son of Henry II. For many years, historians thought that he was a bad king – 'the worst king ever to have sat on the throne'. Here are three things he was accused of doing:

1   He murdered his 16-year-old nephew Arthur in a drunken rage, and threw his body into the river.
     This story was written by a monk-chronicler from Margam Abbey in Glamorgan. Margam Abbey was given money by William de Braose, a great enemy of King John.

2   He tortured and murdered Geoffrey, a priest who criticised him.
     This story was written by Roger of Wendover, a monk-chronicler who was writng after 1230 (John died in 1216). It is known that John made Geoffrey Bishop of Ely, and Geoffrey was still alive in 1225, years after John's death.

3   He gave orders that his wife's lovers had to be strangled on her bed.
     This was written by Matthew Paris, a monk-chronicler writing in 1250.

Do you believe these accusations? In the Middle Ages, all the books were written by monks. In 1208, King John had quarrelled with the Church, so most monks hated him. Did the monks exaggerate his faults? King John certainly had a bad reputation, but did he deserve it?

Many historians would say that he did. Here are some of John's failures that are undeniable facts:

4   He lost Normandy, which was conquered by Philip II, king of France.
5   He lost his quarrel with the Church, and had to accept the Pope as his overlord.
6   He lost his quarrel with the barons, and had to accept the Magna Carta (see pages 46–47).
7   In 1216, Louis Capet, Philip II's son, invaded England.

Left: This picture from Matthew Paris's *Chronicle* shows people being tortured during the reign of King John.

King John

This is a typical description of King John. Make a list of all the words which describe what kind of person John was (there are at least a dozen).

A cold-hearted, selfish man sat alone in a quiet room in a palace, and his thoughts were cunning and bad. It was John, the king who, by his weakness and foolishness, would unite the whole nation against him. During the 17 years of his reign John had three great quarrels.

5   The first was with the King of France. In fighting with him, John lost Normandy altogether.

    John's second quarrel was with the Church. At last the Pope said that John was king no longer and he threw him out of the Church. This scared John so much that he gave in utterly.

10   John's third and worst quarrel was with his own subjects. His cruelty and selfishness lost him the support of the whole nation. His cowardice in the affair with the Pope disgusted them. He tried to bully his nobles, but in this, too, he failed. They drew up the Magna Carta and demanded that the king should sign it. The king was helpless to stop them.

15   *Newnes Pictorial Knowledge, a children's encyclopaedia written in the 1930s.*

Right: This picture from the time shows King John with his dogs. Does it support the monks' claim that John was an inhuman monster?

Modern historians think very differently about John. One of them, Maurice Ashley, has written the following things about King John:

1 He was a hard-working king, who travelled round the whole country even in winter.
2 He was the first king to keep proper records of government documents.
3 He improved the law courts, and made the barons obey the law.
4 He was a faithful Christian, and gave money to the Church and to the poor.
5 He was a good army commander.

The Magna Carta

During 1214, about forty of John's barons complained about the way the king was running the country. They demanded changes in the government.

5 When John heard what they were asking (in April 1215), he refused to agree. 'Why not ask for my kingdom?' he replied angrily.

The barons, led by Robert 10 fitzWalter, called themselves 'The Army of God and the Church'. They marched on London. Some traitors opened the gates for them. The rebels went in and looted the city.

15 John did not want a war with his barons. On 15 June 1215 he met them at Runnymede meadow, on the south bank of the River Thames near Windsor Castle. There he signed the 20 Magna Carta (the Great Charter) – a list of 63 promises.

Over the years, the Magna Carta has been changed and re-written. In the civil wars of the seventeenth century, Parliament used it as an 25 excuse to go to war against King Charles I. It became the basis of Britain's freedom and democracy.

But at the time, in 1215, nobody knew how important it would 30 become. John did not keep his promises. By August 1215 the two sides were at war.

John was attacked on all sides. The Welsh and the Scots invaded England. 35 Some of the barons invited Louis Capet, son of Philip II of France, to take the throne. In the spring of 1216, Louis landed in Kent. John rushed about the country, fighting his 40 enemies, but he became ill and died on 18 October 1216.

This picture of King John signing the Magna Carta was 45 painted in the nineteenth century. It now hangs in the Houses of Parliament. How 50 does the picture depict the event as a disaster for John?

The Magna Carta

The Magna Carta contained 63 promises. Some of the most important promises are listed below.

1 The English Church shall be free to choose its own bishops and archbishops.
2 A baron's son shall inherit his lands on payment to the king of £100, and no more.
10 The king cannot take a tax unless the barons and bishops agree to it in the Great Council.
20 People found guilty in a court of law will not have to pay huge fines for small crimes.
28 No government official can take the corn, horses, carts or wood of a freeman unless that freeman agrees.
39 No freeman shall be arrested or imprisoned without a proper trial by his equals according to the laws of the land.
40 The king cannot sell, deny or delay justice to anyone.
41 All merchants shall be free to travel and trade where they want, without having to pay tolls.
49 The king will immediately return all the hostages he took to make people support him.
51 The king will send out of England all the foreign knights and soldiers he hired.

The Magna Carta, 15 June 1215

? ? ? QUESTION ? ? ?

The barons made John promise not to do the things which had annoyed them.

Look at the list above. Work out TEN things that had made the barons angry.

The Reign of King John

When King John inherited the throne, he ruled a small empire, but he faced many problems.

1 King William 'the Lion' of Scotland wanted to conquer Northumberland.

2 The barons in Ireland were growing too powerful.

3 King Llewelyn of Gwynedd in north Wales was growing very powerful and wanted to take over all of Wales.

4 The English barons were growing too powerful.

5 The government was in a muddle because Richard I had spent so much time on crusade. He had emptied the royal treasury to pay for his wars.

6 The Church was growing too powerful.

7 Until 1204, Normandy was ruled by John. But the Norman barons hated John. In 1201, they rebelled.

8 King Philip II of France wanted to conquer Normandy, so he helped the Norman barons fight against John.

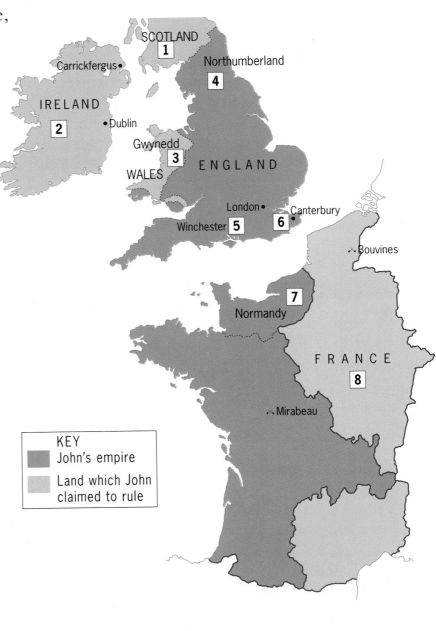

KEY
John's empire
Land which John claimed to rule

Right: This picture from the *Chronicle* of Matthew Paris shows Louis Capet invading England in 1216.

The Events of King John's Reign

December 1199	John collected a new land tax from the knights and the barons. He modernised the government and the law courts.
1 August 1202	John defeated the rebel Norman barons at the battle of Mirabeau.
November 1204	John built Dublin Castle and improved the law courts in Ireland.
April 1205	Philip II of France defeated the English army and drove the English out of Normandy.
August 1209	John built up his forces in the north of England and frightened the Scots into making a peace treaty.
November 1209	John was in the middle of a quarrel with the Pope about who should be Archbishop of Canterbury. Since 1207, the English Church had refused to hold any baptisms, weddings or church services ('the Interdict'). In 1209, the Pope excommunicated John (he threw him out of the Church). In return, John confiscated Church property.
July 1210	John captured Carrickfergus Castle and took control of Ireland.
July 1211	John invaded and conquered Wales.
15 May 1213	John feared that the French were about to invade, so he came to an agreement with the Pope. He accepted the Pope as his overlord, and promised to pay him a tribute of £666 a year.
30 May 1213	John had built a large navy which destroyed the French fleet before it could invade England.
27 July 1214	John invaded Normandy, but was defeated by Philip II of France at the battle of Bouvines.
April 1215	The English barons revolted because of John's demands for money. They captured London.
15 June 1215	The English barons forced John to sign the Magna Carta.
October 1215	The Scots invaded the north of England.
December 1215	The Welsh re-conquered Wales and invaded England.
May 1216	Louis Capet of France invaded England.

The Story of Parliament

Britain is a democracy. Its laws are made by Parliament. Its people choose their government and have the right to change it five years later if they do not like the way they are being ruled.

The story of Parliament began in the Middle Ages. Since then Britain's democracy has grown slowly, over hundreds of years. These pages tell that story. 5

1066   The Great Council
Three times a year – at Christmas, Easter and Whitsuntide – William of Normandy called a Great Council.

The Great Council was made up of barons and bishops. The king asked them for advice, but he could ignore them if he wanted to.

1295   The Model Parliament
King Edward I (1272-1307) asked commoners (knights and rich townspeople), as well as barons, to attend Parliament. They met in the 'House of Commons'. The barons and bishops met in the 'House of Lords'. The king decided when Parliament would meet, and he could still ignore Parliament's advice. 10

1399   Freedom of speech
In 1399, Henry IV gave Parliament freedom of speech (MPs had the right to say whatever they wanted without fear of punishment). 15

Parliament's power was growing. After 1430 every freeman who earned more than £2 a year (quite a lot of money in those days) had the right to vote in elections. 20

1500   The Tudors
The painting on the left shows Henry VIII opening Parliament in 1523. By the time of Henry VIII, the king needed Parliament to pass an 'Act of Parliament' if he wanted to change the law. 25

1689   The Bill of Rights

In 1642, Parliament went to war against King Charles I. In 1649, after the war, Parliament executed him!

In the years after 1660, the first political parties grew up. They were known as the Tories (later to become the Conservative Party) and the Whigs (later to become the Liberal Party).

In 1688, Parliament invited William of Orange to come from Holland to become king. In return, William had to agree to the Bill of Rights (1689). This said that:

- only Parliament could make laws;
- the king could not keep an army;
- the king could not raise his own taxes – each year he was given an income by Parliament, called 'the civil list';
- the people had the right to elect a new Parliament every seven years.

Britain became a 'constitutional monarchy' (there were limits to the power of the king).

1714   Cabinet government

George I, from Hanover in Germany, became king in 1714. He could not speak English. Instead of dealing directly with Parliament, he appointed a 'Prime Minister' to look after Parliament for him. The Prime Minister (not the king) chose a group of ministers who made up 'the Cabinet'. The party which won the most seats in Parliament at the general election ruled the country together with the king.

1832   The Reform Act

The number of people allowed to vote was increased in 1832 and 1867. In 1884, all men over 21 got the vote, and in 1872 the Ballot Act gave people the right to vote in secret. In 1918, women were given the vote for the first time.

Below: Today, the House of Commons makes the laws, and the House of Lords discusses them and suggests changes. The Queen merely signs the laws which Parliament makes.

① Members' gallery
② Government back-benchers
③ Press Gallery
④ The Speaker
⑤ Prime Minister
⑥ Leader of the Opposition
⑦ Opposition back-benchers
⑧ Opposition benches
⑨ Government benches

51

WAR

When a Knight Won His Spurs

In the Middle Ages the knight played a very important role in society. He was the local lord, and the backbone of the king's army. What was he like?

1 Chaucer's knight

There was a KNIGHT, a most respected man,
Who from the day on which he first began
To ride had followed chivalry,
Truth, duty, generosity and courtesy.
5   He had done bravely in his country's wars
And ridden into battle, no man more:
To fifteen deadly battles he had been sent
And jousted for his faith at tournaments . . . .
He was of greatest worth in everybody's eyes.
10 Yet though he was famous, he was wise
And in his manners modest as a maid.
He never yet a nasty thing had said
In all his life to anyone, come what might;
He was a true, a perfect gentle knight.

15 **Geoffrey Chaucer**, *The Canterbury Tales (c. 1386), a poem about a group of pilgrims on their way to Canterbury.*

2 Sir Geoffrey Luttrell is handed his helmet and shield by his wife and daughter. Is he going to joust at a tournament? Or is he riding off to war?

3 The knight's code

When a young noble became a knight,
he had to behave nobly:

You must lead a new life:
Keeping watch in prayer,
Running away from sin, pride and
    wrong-doing;
5 Defending the Church,
Helping the widow and the orphan.

Be bold and protect the people.
Be loyal and brave, taking nothing
    from others.
10 This is how a knight should behave.

He should be humble of heart
And do deeds of chivalry;
He should go to tournaments
    and joust for his lady-love.
15   **Eustace Deschamps**, *a fourteenth-century poet.*

5 A knighting ceremony in the twelfth century. The knight promises obedience to the king, and is given his sword and spurs. This knight has 'won his spurs' by his bravery in battle.

4 Courtly love

It was fashionable for a knight to
fall in love with a married lady. He
devoted his life to her, longing for a
love he could never have:

I serve the fairest lady
In the world (and say so openly).
I am hers from head to toe,
And even in cold winds
5 The love raining in my heart
Keeps me warm.

My heart burns and breaks for her:
And if she does not heal me
With a kiss before the new year,
10 I will die . . . .

I am Arnaut who gathers the wind
And chases rabbits on an ox
And swims against the incoming tide.
      Arnaut Daniel (*c.1200*).
15   *Arnaut was a knight and a wandering*
minstrel (singer).

6 A twelfth-century tournament. Knights joust while their ladies watch.

Feasting

In the Middle Ages, rich people loved to have feasts. A generous knight invited many guests, and gave them so much food that the table almost
5 collapsed under the weight.

Tables were usually just boards laid across trestles, covered with a cloth. People in very wealthy households ate from wooden platters (plates), but
10 usually food was put on slices of bread called trenchers. The bread was cut by a servant called a panter.

Etiquette

Everything had to be done with great ceremony. On the table there would
15 be a salt nef – a huge salt-cellar in the shape of a ship. Important guests sat 'above the salt'; less important guests sat lower down, 'below the salt'. Fights would break out if
20 someone tried to sit at a higher place than he or she deserved.

There were strict rules about how to behave at feasts. Etiquette (good manners) was essential. Most people
25 ate with their fingers, as forks were not used very much in the Middle Ages. Certain fingers were used to hold certain foods, and hands were carefully washed between courses.
30 Meals were organised by a servant called the chamberlain. In some houses a servant called the groom of the hall carried in the dishes and took away the dirty plates. In very
35 wealthy households, however, meals were served by the sons of

neighbouring knights, who had been placed in the lord's household to learn how to behave. Carving the meat was the most skilled task, and 40 the carver was the son of the lord himself, or a favourite servant. A butler poured the wine.

Meals

A big meal might have three or four courses. Each course would include 45 up to ten different dishes, which were eaten in turn.

People ate such things as porpoise, minnows, tripe, peacocks and swans. Cooks liked to give the guests surprise 50 dishes – for instance, a pie containing four-and-twenty blackbirds, which flew out when the pie was opened, or a dish full of frogs, which hopped across the table when the lid was 55 lifted. Between each course, servants carried in a 'subtlety' – a food sculpture in the shape of a saint, for instance.

During meals, guests were often 60 entertained by musicians, jugglers, acrobats and jesters. Pets wandered about the table. Sometimes, platters had rude or romantic poems written on them. At the end of the feast, 65 guests had to make up a tune and sing the verses on their plate.

As each dish was served, some of the food was put to one side. At the end of the meal this – together with 70 all the leftovers – was given to the poor people of the village.

Below: Jean, Duc de Berry, holds a feast to exchange New Year gifts, in about 1415. Can you see him, seated at the head of the table?

Can you see the great fireplace (with the fire burning behind a screen), an aumbry (a cupboard for the cups and serving plates), a tapestry hanging on the wall, the table, the tablecloth, a huge nef, pet dogs on the table, a man in a blue cloak with two mazers (wooden drinking cups), and some round wooden platters on the table?

Can you also see a man using certain fingers to hold the food? Can you find the carver, the butler, and the chamberlain (with a stick) inviting the guests to 'Approche (come in)'?

Historians think that the guest wearing a floppy light-blue hat is Paul de Limbourg, the artist who painted the picture.

Kings at War

In times of peace, knights enjoyed feasting and hunting, but their main job was to fight in the king's army. During much of the Middle Ages, England was at war with its neighbours. English people often portray the English kings of this time as heroic warriors. To the Irish, Welsh, Scots and French, it must have seemed that they were nasty trouble-makers!

Ireland

Henry II invaded Ireland in 1171. Throughout the Middle Ages, the kings of England gave Irish land to English barons. They tried to force the Irish to speak English and to obey English laws and customs (such as having a bath). They failed.

This Irish lord has decided to take a bath, but he and his followers are eating raw horsemeat!

The Irish lords rebelled again and again. English families who went to live in Ireland adopted Irish ways. By 1450 the English only ruled a small area round Dublin called the Pale.

Wales

Llewelyn ap Gruffudd, the ruler of Gwynedd, was the grandson of Llewelyn the Great – who had given King John so much trouble (see page 48). Llewelyn started to call himself the Prince of Wales.

In 1277, King Edward I invaded and conquered Gwynedd. He built a number of strong castles such as Beaumaris Castle. Llewelyn was killed in 1282. He is known as 'Llewelyn the Last'.

This painting from the 1930s glamorises a famous story from Welsh history. Edward I promised the Welsh a prince of their own, who would be born in Wales and would not be able to speak English. In 1284, while Edward I was in Wales, his son Edward was born. According to legend, the king showed the baby to the people. 'Here is your prince,' he said. 'He was born in Wales and can speak no English.' Even today, the heir to the throne is called the Prince of Wales.

In reality, Edward was not declared Prince of Wales until 1301. He had spent little of his childhood in Wales.

The Hollywood film *Braveheart* tells the story of Wallace, but it is full of historical errors! 80

Scotland

King Edward I also tried to conquer Scotland. In 1296, he invaded.

The Scots resisted. They were led by William Wallace.

55 Wallace was captured and executed, but in 1306 another Scot, Robert Bruce, claimed the Scottish crown. He was defeated many times, but he kept on trying.

60 In 1307, Edward I died. On his grave were written the words: 'Edward, the Hammer of the Scots.' But his son Edward II was not as strong, and Bruce totally defeated
65 him at the battle of Bannockburn (1314).

In 1320, the Scots published The Declaration of Arbroath. It said:

As long as 100 men remain alive, we
70 shall never accept English rule. It is not for glory or riches that we are fighting, but for freedom.

France

In 1337 King Edward III went to war with France. Fighting went on (with
75 lulls in between) for more than a century. This is called the Hundred Years' War.

At that time, the English longbow was the most deadly weapon of the age. The English won great victories at the battles of Crécy (1346), Poitiers (1356) and Agincourt (1415). At times 85 they controlled most of France. But the kings of England did not have strong enough armies to keep control of France. In 1453, they were finally driven out, although they still owned 90 the port of Calais.

According to legend, a peasant girl called Joan of Arc (on the left of the picture) inspired the French armies to drive out the English. Joan of Arc was a real person, but the invention of the cannon 95 probably played a more important part in the French victory, because the French could capture the English castles.

Castles

Barons of the Middle Ages built castles to defend themselves against the enemy.

1 This scene from the Bayeux tapestry shows Dinant castle in Belgium.

After 1066, the Norman barons built motte and bailey castles. The local Saxons were forced to heap up a mound of earth (the motte). A wooden tower called a keep was built on top.

Sometimes there was a courtyard called the bailey at the bottom of the mound. It was surrounded by a wall of wooden stakes. In the bailey were the stables and barns, the bakehouse, the blacksmith's and the living quarters.

2 A painting of Scarborough Castle in Yorkshire.

After 1100, the barons built huge stone keeps. The walls were up to seven metres thick. Notice the steps up to the main drawbridge.

Why are the windows at the top of the keep larger than those near the bottom? Why is the wall at the bottom of the tower angled outwards?

3 Warkworth Castle, Northumberland.

The crusaders learned a lot about castle design when they were fighting the Muslims in the Holy Land. After 1150, the barons began to build strong curtain walls, defended by towers, around the keep. These were an extra means of defence.

4 Beaumaris Castle, North Wales.

Edward I's castles in Wales were the best of all. They were concentric castles, which means that they had a central courtyard surrounded by more than one wall. Notice that the inner walls are higher than the outer walls. Which part of the castle is most heavily defended?

Notice that the towers are round. Why were round towers better than square towers?

59

Besieged!

The pictures on pages 60–63 are from the period 1250–1500. They show the kinds of things that happened during a siege in the Middle Ages.

1 An army prepares to set off to war.

2 An army camp during a siege. The baggage wagons are on the outside. The foot-soldiers' tents are in the inside ring, and the knights' tents are in the centre. Notice the guarded gate on the left, and the bar and gambling tables on the right.

3 An army would first try to take a castle by surprise, making a rush on the gate. What different things are they doing to try to capture the castle? What are the defenders doing?

4 The siege. What are the attackers doing? Notice the siege tower on the left. What have the archers set up (in the centre of the picture) to protect themselves from the arrows being shot by the defenders on the walls? What are the defenders doing?

5 As the siege went on, the defenders would become hungry and they often became ill. They would make surprise attacks from the castle, called sorties. Notice the trebuchet, a large machine for throwing rocks at the castle walls (at the top of the picture).

6 'Once more unto the breach, dear friends,' shouts King Henry in Shakespeare's play *Henry V*. A breach was a gap in the castle walls made by the attackers. The attackers then rushed into the breach to try to take the castle. You can see in the picture what happened next.

7 The attackers have defeated the defenders. What are they doing now?

8 To save their city from further destruction, the townspeople are surrendering the keys of the city to the attackers. If the defenders did not surrender, the attackers had the right to kill every man, woman and child.

Good Knight?

Knights were men of war. Is it really possible that they were all as chivalrous and gentle as they were supposed to be? The sources on these pages give some examples of knights and noblemen behaving badly.

1 Knights in the reign of King Stephen

King Stephen (1135-54) was not strong enough to control his barons and knights. As a result, there was a civil war in England. This is what happened:

They captured any men and women who they thought were rich. They put them into prison and tortured them to make them hand over their gold and silver. They hung them up by the feet and smoked them with foul smoke. They tied knotted rope around their heads and twisted it till it entered their brain. They put them in prisons with adders and snakes and toads, and so killed them . . . .

The Anglo-Saxon Chronicle (1137)

2 Knights attacking unarmed villagers.

3 The crusades

One of the crusader-knights wrote:

I love it when fighting soldiers
scatter the people and herds in their path . . . .
    Let each noble man think of nothing
but breaking heads and arms – I tell you,
I enjoy nothing in food or wine or sleep as much
as hearing the shout of 'At them!' on both sides,
and the cries of 'Help! Help!',
and in seeing the dead.

Bertrand de Born, *a letter-poem written in 1194. Bertrand wrote this letter to King Richard the Lionheart to try to persuade him to go on crusade. When the crusaders captured Jerusalem, they killed so many people that they were wading in blood up to their ankles.*

? QUESTION ?

Why are the knights on these pages so different from the image of the knight on pages 52-53?

4 Edward II and Queen Isabella hated each other. He was homosexual. She and her nobleman lover deposed him, and had him horribly murdered.

5 The Hundred Years' War

During the war, the English army conducted *chevauchées*. The knights burned, looted and killed everything in their path.

Nowadays, the man who does not know how to set places on fire, to rob churches and imprison priests, is not thought fit to wage war. I think it is wrong when a man-at-arms takes a woman and does her shame, or sets fire to a church. In these days all wars are directed against the poor working people. I do not call that war; I call it robbery.

Honoré Bouvet, *Tree of Battles (fifteenth century)*

6 Knights looting a merchant's house.

A CHANGING WORLD

The Bustling Towns

When William conquered England in 1066, only half a dozen places had more than 4,000 people living in them. During the Middle Ages,
5 however, many towns grew up in England. By 1500, Norwich, Bristol and Newcastle had more than 10,000 inhabitants and London probably had 50,000.
10 You would have found a walk through the narrow streets of a town very exciting. Wealthy people were dressed in brightly coloured clothes. The poor wore dull brown and black
15 tunics. Carts piled with wood squeezed past mules loaded with cloth or vegetables. There was constant noise. The town crier competed with the shouts of shopkeepers and street-
20 sellers, with the church bells, and with the huge shop signs which squeaked in the wind.

However, towns were cruel and violent places. People laughed at
25 beggars and cripples. A quarrel over a road accident or litter often ended in a fight, and in somebody's death.

At 8 p.m. a bell rang for curfew, when everyone was supposed to shut
30 up their houses and go to bed.

A town street in fourteenth-century France. Compare it to a modern street.

The Streets of London

Then to London I did me hie;   hie: go
  Of all the land it bears the prize.
'Hot peascods,' one began to cry;   peascods: pea-pods
  'Strawberries ripe,' others ask me and advise.
5   One bade me come near and buy some spice;   bade: asked
Pepper and saffron they me plead.   saffron: a yellow food-flavouring
But for lack of money I could not speed.   speed: to be happy in life

Then to Cheapside I went on,
  Where many people I saw to stand.
10 One offered me velvet, silk and linen;
  Another took me by the hand,
  'Here is Paris thread, the finest in the land.'
I never was used to such things indeed,
And lacking money, I could not speed.

15 Then I went out by London Stone,   Stone: milestone
  Through all Candlewick Street;
Drapers much cloth offered me anon.   drapers: cloth-sellers
  Then I met one who cried, 'Hot sheep's feet.'
  One cried, 'Fish';
20 'Rushes green,' another gan greet.   gan greet: gave a greeting
One bade me buy a hood to cover my head;
But for lack of money I could not speed.

Then I hied me into Eastcheap;
  One cried, 'Ribs of beef and many a pie.'
25 Pewter pots they clattered on a heap;
  There was harp, pipe and minstrels there.   minstrels: singers
  'Yes, old friend!' 'Nay, my friend!' some began to cry;
Some sang of St Julian for their meed,   meed: wages
But for lack of money I could not speed.   St Julian: a saint famous
                                 for his generosity

30 Then to Westminster gate I presently went,
  When the sun was at high prime.   high prime: 9 a.m.
Cooks on me they were all intent,
  And offered me bread, with ale and wine;
  Ribs of beef, both fat and full fine;
35 A fair cloth they began for to spread,
But lacking money I could not be sped.

John Lydgate, *London Lickpenny (early fifteenth century)*

Dirty Old Town

The Guilds

Many towns began as marketplaces where local farmers took surplus food to sell. As time went on, traders set up shops there, and craftsmen started up
5 small industries.

People of the same trade tended to live in the same street, which is why we still have streets with names such as Baker Street and Goldsmiths' Lane.
10 Traders formed clubs called guilds. The guilds made sure that their products were well made and that the traders charged fair prices. They also looked after members who had fallen
15 on hard times.

A young person who wanted to learn a trade became an apprentice with a master craftsman. The child worked for the master, and the master
20 gave the apprentice 'clothes, bedding, food and beatings'. After seven years, the youth became a skilled employee, called a journeyman (because he was paid by the day – in French, *par*
25 *journée*).

After many years, the journeyman submitted a special piece of his work (called his masterpiece) to the guild. If the guild members thought it was
30 good enough, they would acccept him as a master craftsman, and he could set up his own business.

Surnames began to appear in the Middle Ages, and many people were named after their trade –
35 which is why we have surnames such as Carpenter, Miller, Barber and Cook. What surnames came from the trades shown in pictures 1–4?

The Black Death

Death comes into our midst like black smoke,
A plague which cuts off the young,
A rootless ghost which has no mercy for good looks.
Woe is me of the mark in the armpit!
5 It is throbbing, terrible –
A head that gives pain and causes a loud cry,
A painful, angry lump.
Great is its throbbing like a burning coal,
A horrible thing of grey colour –
10 Like the seeds of black peas, or broken bits of sea-coal,
The early jewellery of black death,
A black plague like pennies, like berries.

A Welsh poem (fourteenth century)

The Triumph of Death, a wall-painting by Francesco Traini (*c.* 1350). A hunting party comes across three open coffins. The corpses are rotting. Vipers crawl over them. The smell is terrible. Even the horses and the dogs are scared. 'What you are, we were. What we are, you will be,' the corpses tell the nobles.

In 1348–50 a terrible plague came to the British Isles. Doctors could not cure it. This account of the plague was written using documents from the time:

The coming disaster

a   The plague came from India, through Greece and Italy, and then into France.

b   In 1348, two ships landed in the fishing village of Melcombe in Dorset. The sailors came from France, and they were infected with the plague; they brought the plague to Britain.

The pestilence

c   The plague killed countless people, especially the poor.

d   Few of those who became infected lived longer than three days.

e   Boils and abscesses broke out on people's legs and in their armpits.

f   Other victims got little black pustules all over their whole body.

g   Another symptom was a violent headache, so bad that it drove some people into a frenzy.

h   The plague was so contagious that people who touched the sick seemed to become immediately infected themselves.

i   Some writers guessed that only a tenth of mankind remained alive.

j   It was said that there were hardly enough people left alive to bury the dead.

k   An animal epidemic followed the pestilence.

l   At Kilkenny in Ireland, Brother John Clyn, the last monk left alive in his monastery, wondered if any human being would escape death.

A different world

m   The shortage of workers was so bad that more than a third of the land was left unfarmed. In some places, knights and lords had to farm the land themselves.

n   Poor people became rebellious, bitter and angry. It seemed as though no-one would take orders from anyone.

o   'There was so much sadness,' wrote one chronicler, 'that the world could never return to its former state.'

The Peasants' Revolt

1 On Thursday, 30 May 1381, Thomas Bampton was collecting taxes in Essex.

He treated the villagers of Fobbing badly.

2 Later that day, Thomas the Baker and one hundred villagers attacked Bampton.

5 On Thursday, 13 June 1381, John Ball preached to the rebels:

> GOD CREATED ALL MEN EQUAL. IT IS TIME FOR FREEDOM.

> I LIKE HIM. WE WILL MAKE HIM ARCHBISHOP OF CANTERBURY.

6 Later that day, three merchants opened the gates of London.

They let in the rebels.

9 King Richard II was only 14 years old. On Saturday, 15 June 1381, he met Tyler at Smithfield.

10 Tyler insulted the king.

> NO MORE VILLEINS! ALL MEN MUST BE FREE AND EQUAL.

William of Walworth, the Lord Mayor of London, killed Tyler.

3 Twenty thousand peasants rebelled.

4 *On Friday, 7 June 1381*, the rebels asked Wat Tyler to be their leader.

WE ARE NO LONGER PREPARED TO EAT YESTERDAY'S STALE VEGETABLES!

They marched to London.

8 They went to the Tower of London.

7 The rebels burned the houses of the rich.

The Archbishop of Canterbury, who was the king's adviser, was hiding there. The rebels killed him.

11 Richard spoke to the rebels:

I WILL BE YOUR KING AND YOUR LEADER.

The peasants went home.

12 Many peasants were hanged.

VILLEINS YOU WERE AND VILLEINS YOU WILL STAY.

Why Did the Peasants Revolt?

When Wat Tyler met Richard II at Smithfield on Saturday, 15 June 1381, this is what he demanded:
- the law should not be so harsh;
- there should be no outlaws;
- there should be no lords except the king;
- the wealth of the Church should be shared amongst the poor;
- there should be no more villeins; all men should be free and equal.

QUESTIONS

Why was there a rebellion in 1381? Historians have identified many causes, which you can read about on page 77.
1 Give each cause a suitable title.
2 Put the suggested causes into order of date.
3 Choose the two causes which you think are the most important.

a The villeins hated being villeins. Some had taken their lords to court to get their duties reduced. Others joined together and refused to work for their lords. This had been going on since 1300.

Parliament had recently passed a law to stop this, and to imprison 'all such rebels'.

b On Thursday, 30 May 1381, Thomas Bampton tried to collect the Poll Tax from the villagers of Fobbing in Essex. He threatened the men. He lifted the females' skirts to see if they were women (who had to pay) or girls (who did not). This made the villagers angry and they rioted.

c After the Black Death of 1348–50, poor people became rebellious, bitter and angry. They would not take orders from anybody.

d In March 1381 Parliament sent Commissioners to every village to make everybody pay a Poll Tax. It was the third Poll Tax in four years. The tax was hard on the poor people, who became very angry.

e Since 1377, England had been ruled by a boy-king. At the time of the Peasants' Revolt, Richard II was only 14 years old. This meant that the government was weak, and the peasants felt they had more chance of success.

f In 1351, Parliament had passed a law saying that if a workman asked for a wage rise, he could be outlawed or branded. This made the workers angry.

g On Friday, 7 June 1381, the rebels asked Wat Tyler to be their leader. He was an ex-soldier and a good leader.

i Since 1369, England had been fighting – and losing – a war against France. People were angry and blamed the government.

h Since 1360 a priest called John Ball had criticised wealthy priests and lords. He told the rebels:

> God created all men equal. It is time for freedom. The rulers are the weeds of England, and you must pick out and throw away the evil lords.

The peasants liked him. He encouraged them to rebel.

j The merchants and traders of London hated each other. They supported the rebellion because they hoped that the peasants would kill their enemies.

On Thursday, 13 June 1381, three of them opened the gates of London for the rebels.

Into the Future

According to the chronicler Thomas Walsingham, after the Peasants' Revolt, Richard II told the rebels:

> Villeins you were and villeins you will
> 5 stay – not as before, but worse. Your slavery will be an example to others.

Richard probably never said this (Walsingham was copying a story in the Bible) but – even if he did – the
10 saying turned out to be wrong. Most lords realised that the revolt was (in the words of a poem of the time) 'a warning to beware'. **Lords began to set their villeins free**. A century
15 later, there were no villeins in England.

During the fifteenth century, other events were changing England, completely and for ever.
20 **Warfare was changed by the use of gunpowder**. As no castle was strong enough to withstand a cannon bombardment, no nobleman was strong enough to ignore the king.
25 At the same time, the nobles of England became involved in **the Wars of the Roses**. Unlike other wars in the Middle Ages, the Wars of the Roses had little effect on ordinary
30 people, but they bankrupted and ruined the nobles.

Meanwhile, **a new middle class of merchants and traders** was becoming powerful. Trade grew in
35 the fifteenth century. **Improvements in ships and navigation** allowed sailors to go further, faster. English wool was in demand all over the known world. Eventually, an Italian explorer called **Columbus crossed** 40 **the Atlantic Ocean and reached America**. You may have heard the rhyme:

> In fourteen hundred and ninety-two, Columbus sailed the ocean blue, 45

but did you know that some historians think that sailors from Bristol in England discovered America *before* Columbus – but decided to keep their profitable discovery a secret! 50

A picture painted during the Middle Ages.

Also during the fifteenth century, there were advances in painting. By the sixteenth century, artists knew how to draw in perspective, so their pictures seemed more lifelike.

Man's knowledge of science improved. An astronomer called **Galileo said that the sun did NOT go round the earth** (as the Roman Catholic Church taught). He realised that the earth went round the sun.

Other people began to undermine the power of the Church. **Scholars who studied the Greek language discovered mistakes in the Latin version of the Bible** used by the Roman Catholic Church.

A picture painted by Leonardo da Vinci in 1526.

Meanwhile, **the invention of the printing press** allowed printers to produce books much more quickly and cheaply than the monks had ever been able to do, copying them out by hand. Books are dangerous things! The new ideas spread across Europe like a new plague, infecting people's minds, and killing off old ideas and institutions.

It was a time of Renaissance (meaning 'rebirth') – a time when civilisation moved forward quickly.

Have you ever wondered why the Middle Ages are called the 'Middle Ages'? The people of the Renaissance were very pleased with themselves. They admitted that the Roman Empire was brilliant. They believed that they were brilliant. But they thought that everything in between was second-rate. A Renaissance historian, Flavio Biondo, decided to call those years 'the Middle Ages' – the low point in between the Roman Empire and the Renaissance.

??? QUESTION ???

The people of the Renaissance dismissed the Middle Ages as a time of unhappiness, bad rulers and feeble ideas.

You have studied the Middle Ages in this book. Do you agree with them?

INDEX